BORROWED WISDOM
That Made Me Wise

BORROWED WISDOM
That Made Me Wise

Dr. Vartika Dikshit

PAPER TOWNS
PUBLISHERS

PAPER TOWNS
PUBLISHERS

First published by

Papertowns Publishers
72, Vishwanath Dham Colony,
Niwaru Road, Jhotwara,
Jaipur, 302012

Borrowed Wisdom That Made Me Wise

ISBN Print Book – 978-93-6185-268-8

Printed in India

DEDICATION

To Mamma—

The eternal optimist, the most pragmatic soul, the wisest guide, and the most progressive woman I have ever known.

If wisdom had a voice, it would sound like you. If resilience had a face, it would look like you. And if love had a definition, it would simply be *Mamma*.

I have borrowed so much from you—your strength, grace, and ability to find light even in the darkest corners. But I will be honest—no words, pages, or ink can ever fully capture the depth of what you've given me.

And now, life has come full circle. My daughter says she wants to grow up to be a mom like Nani because, in her words, "*Nani did a better job than you, Mamma*". So here I am, scratching my head, wondering how to take that. But honestly, it proves what I've always known—you're everything to both of us…Perfect.

Introduction

Books have always been a constant companion in my life, whether as a refuge, a source of inspiration, or simply a reason to smile on an otherwise mundane day. This is my second book, and in many ways, it is why I wrote my first with such joy, humour, and pleasantness. If the first book reflects my thoughts and experiences, this one is a tribute to the words that shaped them.

WHY THIS BOOK?

In my 45 years on this planet, books have played a pivotal role in my journey. From *Heidi* by Johanna Spyri to *Wuthering Heights*, my life as a student was often viewed through the lens of the books I picked up from the school library.

Over the years, books have been more than just stories or knowledge; they have been my sanctuary. During times of crisis, when I needed peace, calm, and guidance, and when seeking professional help was either financially or logistically challenging, books stepped in as my silent counsellors. Their words have comforted me in moments of distress, motivated me in times of self-doubt, and even made me laugh when I needed it the most.

THE HABIT THAT LED TO THIS COMPILATION

I have a simple habit—I underline passages that speak to me while reading. Some lines resonate so profoundly that they linger in my thoughts long after I have turned the last page. I now share these quotes with you in this book. These words have guided me over the last few years, challenged my perspective, and offered clarity when I felt lost. I hope that they do the same for you.

To make this collection more accessible, I have categorized the quotes into themes for easy reference. Life, after all, does not come with a manual, but these words have often served as guideposts in my journey. We all experience nervousness, fear, and confusion—reading has been my way of navigating through them.

This book is my way of expressing gratitude to the authors who have unknowingly been my mentors. Their wisdom has helped me navigate different roles, solve dilemmas, and find answers that no self-help guide could provide. Through this compilation, I pass on their insights in the hope that they bring the same peace, joy, and clarity to you as they have to me.

Why 45?

I was pleasantly overwhelmed after diving into numerous books and jotting down quotes that resonated long after reading. Each quote encapsulated a fragment of someone else's journey while reflecting my experiences.

When it came time to select my favourites, I felt conflicted. Ten felt too few, while a hundred seemed overly ambitious (perhaps a bit self-indulgent). I wanted a number that felt meaningful and deliberate.

Then it hit me—I'm celebrating my 45th birthday this year. What better way to commemorate this milestone than by sharing 45 pieces of wisdom I've gathered? One for each year filled with learning, love, challenges, laughter, tears, and personal growth.

These quotes are more than words; they serve as reminders, companions, and gentle guides. Each one has influenced my perspective or prompted me to take a moment to reflect more deeply on myself.

So here they are—45 quotes for 45 years. A gift to myself, and now, to you.

Enjoy your reading!

Reflections

HOPE, RESILIENCE, STRENGTH, SELF-GROWTH

1. Grit

Angela Duckworth, Pg 203

"Grit depends on a different kind of hope. It rests on the expectation that our own efforts can improve our future. I have a feeling tomorrow will be better is different from I resolve to make tomorrow better. The hope that gritty people have has nothing to do with luck and everything to do with getting up again."

Every setback presents a chance for a comeback. True resilience lies in the ability to rise again, regardless of how often you fall.

I've encountered rejections and unexpected changes. Yet, each misstep has become a stepping stone toward something greater. Consistency triumphs over perfection.

From being a class topper to being a housewife for 14 years to starting a professional journey in my late thirties, it was not easy changing gears, but every challenge came with an opportunity. Giving up was not a choice I wanted to give to myself. From living in the shadows to having a vast professional network and an identity in the industry was something that I had never imagined, but it happened.

The journey to success is seldom straightforward, filled with twists, turns, and uncertainties. However, each obstacle teaches us something valuable. With every failure, we have the opportunity to rebuild even stronger.

Growth emerges from discomfort, and reinvention is born from challenges. The most compelling stories are found in the chapters on resilience.

Can you share a time when you transformed a setback into a comeback?

RESILIENCE TURNS SETBACKS INTO STEPPING STONES FOR SUCCESS.

2. Britt-Marie Was Here

Frederick Backman, Pg 241

"Jump, Britt-Marie! Just jump! You have to understand that when one is just standing there looking, then just for a second one is ready to jump. If one does it, one dares to do it. But if one waits, it'll never happen."

Overthinking can hinder progress while taking risks fosters personal development. Some of my most impactful choices stemmed from taking a leap of faith instead of waiting for the ideal moment. Waiting for that 'perfect' moment often leads to endless delays.

At 36, I began my career as an intern at a prestigious PR agency, facing the challenge of working alongside much younger colleagues straight out of school. I had two options: I could either dwell on my age and life circumstances or seize this opportunity that could launch my professional path. I opted for the latter and am grateful I didn't back out. It has been a rewarding journey of continuous growth and progress. The second career opportunity required me to commute for hours every day and literally "climb up the mountains", which gave me more nausea than the two pregnancies but not only did it make me mentally strong and get me recognition at work, it got me my third break based on the commitment I showed in the previous one.

GROWTH HAPPENS WHEN YOU LEAP, NOT WHEN YOU WAIT.

3. The Boy, the Mole, the Fox and the Horse

Charlie Mackesy

"One of our greatest freedoms is how we react to things."

Although we can't dictate every situation, we can always choose how we react. I've discovered that my true strength comes from my reactions rather than the occurring events. It's also worth noting that sometimes, choosing not to respond can be the most powerful response. Keeping quiet is not always a sign of weakness; knowing when not to respond is a virtue of people who know exactly what needs their attention, time, and energy. More than proving a point, it is important to save yourself from the stress that you might invite by responding or reacting.

At one of the meetings with my boss, I was told, "I have a husband and in-laws to look after, I can't check your work after 6 pm."

It did not sit well with me – it was an indirect way of targeting my marital status.

The next morning, I was quiet during the call, quiet during the afternoon call, and by evening, my boss called and apologized.

As adults, we are all aware of what we say. I did not keep quiet because I was a subordinate; I felt a verbal argument would make me cross the boundary, but keeping quiet would be a civilized way of protest.

Ultimately, it is important to be mindful of what we choose – no response/ reaction, indifference, silence, or communication because it would affect us more than anybody else. My priority is -PEACE OF MIND. I plan my responses accordingly.

TRUE STRENGTH DOES NOT LIE IN REACTING.

4. Believe in the God Who Believes in You

Robert H. Schuller, Pg 31

"What happens to people who meet people who believe in them? Miracles, as we shall see. Miracles!"

The power of belief and encouragement can transform lives. Having someone who believes in you can create the confidence to achieve great things. I've been lucky to have mentors and teams who believed in my vision, whether in hospitality or academia. Their faith in me made me push boundaries, and I try to do the same for those around me.

My first boss hired me when I had zero work experience; he showed faith in my conversational and writing abilities while ignoring that I had never worked and was a housewife for 14 years. That faith helped me create magic…there was no looking back.

BELIEVING AND TRUSTING RESULTS IN MIRACLES.

5. The Fakir

Ruzbeh N. Bharucha, Pg 114

"Destiny is a road map that points out the general direction, major destinations and gives an overview of the journey to be undertaken. Avoiding potholes, bad roads and speed breakers and using common sense are at the discretion of the driver."

Fate may lay the groundwork, but it's our individual decisions that define the path we take. We hold the reins when it comes to facing life's hurdles.

While having a plan is essential, being flexible is crucial. Achieving success relies on our ability to adjust and maneuver around difficulties.

In 2022, I applied to the US for a third Master's Program (Business Analytics). I got accepted at 7 out of 9 universities where I applied. I resigned from work, left one child in India, and took the younger one with me. The drill did not end there: I had to manage a home, two part-time jobs at the University, and my studies. Soon, I realized I had made a bad decision - I would end up in massive debt with no job security once the course was over. Moreover, it was something that did not interest me. It had been 2 months since I had moved to the US, but I had to control the damage now. I did not care about social shaming back in my country. Just spoke with my children and shared why I was planning to drop out, and like always, they said, "We trust you, Mamma." I began packing and selling everything I had bought while requesting my dean for a course I could do remotely and looking for a job back home because the paycheck needed to keep coming. I landed in India with a job and enrolled in a course more suitable for my professional growth, which I completed in 2023.

BEING FLEXIBLE HELPS IN NAVIGATING TOUGH TIMES.

6. Who Will Cry When You Die?

Robin Sharma, Pg 118

"But just as a rocket uses more fuel during the first few minutes after lift-off than it does over the days that follow when it will cover more than half a million miles, once you get past those first 21 days you will find that staying on course with a new habit will be far easier than you imagined."

The most challenging aspect of change is getting started. Once a habit takes root, it becomes much easier to maintain. Beginning is often the toughest hurdle to overcome, but the journey becomes more manageable as you gain momentum.

When I first entered the workforce, I wasn't accustomed to spending long hours on a laptop and often felt drowsy after lunch since I was used to napping. I also tried to connect with colleagues significantly younger than me, as I had started my career later in life. Looking back after seven years, I can't imagine a day without work, and my younger teammates have always made me feel youthful.

The hardest part of change is the beginning. Once a habit is established, sustaining it becomes easier.

Starting is always the hardest part. But once momentum builds, the path gets smoother.

THE BEST TIME TO CHANGE A HABIT IS NOW.

7. Time to Come Home

Damini Grover, Pg 123-124

"We create stories and interpretations about everything, especially ourselves. Then why not create the ones that are uplifting and empowering?"

The narratives we create for ourselves significantly influence our lives. By altering your story, you can transform your reality.

I understand that the way we tell our stories can shift our perspectives. This principle also holds in life—revise your narrative to empower yourself.

When I went through my divorce, many people expressed their condolences, saying, "I'm so sorry to hear that." I would respond, "Couples separate because they're unhappy together; no one has passed away, so why the 'sorry'?" This has always been my viewpoint; others keep pitying you until you don't stop pitying yourself.

YOU HAVE THE POWER TO CHANGE YOUR NARRATIVE. DO IT.

8. Many Lives, Many Masters

Dr. Brian Weiss, Pg 112

"Patience and timing…everything comes when it must come. A life cannot be rushed, cannot be worked on a schedule as so many people want it to be. We must accept what comes to us at a given time and not ask for more."

Life is not a straightforward path; rather, it is a continuous cycle of learning, growth, and transformation. Our existence goes beyond the limits of time and physical form — we are souls on an everlasting journey, each lifetime serving as a classroom and every challenge acting as a teacher. Genuine peace arises from having patience and faith in this journey.

There were times when I felt the urge to hasten outcomes, reach goals quickly, or question the delays I faced. However, reflecting on my experiences, I realize that every stage imparted vital lessons necessary for the next chapter. My career decisions, educational endeavours, and personal development have all unfolded at the right moments, even if I couldn't recognize them then. This quote is a reassuring reminder: there's no need to rush the Universe. What truly matters is patience, trust, and the willingness to learn — and that life, in all its forms, continues to progress, just as I do.

After my son was born, I experienced three miscarriages. I longed for another child, driven by the desire to avoid a significant age gap between them. It became a matter of ego for me. My daughter arrived after considerable struggle and years of waiting. I feel immense gratitude towards the Universe when I consider the bigger picture. I separated from my ex-husband when my second child was just five, and my elder one was twelve. If their ages had been closer, I would have faced considerable financial strain while trying to support their education as I began my career. My son is in college, and my daughter is still in school. By the time she is ready for college, I will have the support of my son.

EVERYTHING COMES WHEN IT MUST COME.

LOVE, MARRIAGE, RELATIONSHIPS

9. Reflections of a Man

Amari Soul

Pg 140

"The most important impression a man can make on you is not the first impression, but rather a lasting impression that only comes from consistency over time."

Pg 160

"The right man won't want you to lower your standards; he would rather push himself to meet or exceed them."

First impressions may dazzle, but they can fade quickly. What truly matters — and what stays with us — is consistency. The quiet repetition of values, actions, and reliability over time leaves a lasting mark. In relationships, work, or leadership, anyone can impress one; the ones who truly stand out are those who keep showing up with the same integrity day after day.

Over the years, I've learned that charm and showmanship are fleeting. Consistency is what earns trust, whether in teams, friendships, or life. It's not about the grand gestures or carefully curated first moments. It's about showing up with the same sincerity and reliability every time. The most impressive people aren't those who impress once but those whose steadiness becomes their signature. That's who I strive to be and surround myself with.

Love isn't about grand gestures but about consistency and reliability. Authentic love reveals itself in sustained effort rather than fleeting charm.

I've always believed that relationships, like brands, are built on trust and repeated positive experiences. Just like marketing campaigns can't survive on a one-time viral post, love needs long-term effort to leave a lasting impact.

A healthy relationship challenges you to grow rather than making you settle.

Like in leadership, the right partnership is about mutual growth. The best relationships—personal or professional—push us forward, not hold us back.

TRUE IMPACT IS BUILT ON STEADY INTEGRITY.

10. Spouse

Shobhaa De, Pg 66

"Living through a spell of 'foul weather' in a marriage is one thing; living with a 'foul person' quite another."

Rough patches should not be confused with toxic relationships. This distinction extends beyond marriage; it also pertains to friendships, business partnerships, and workplace dynamics. While a temporary crisis can be addressed and managed, a toxic environment is far more challenging. Recognizing this difference is crucial.

REMEMBER- Behavioural problems can often be resolved with support, counselling, and intervention, whereas character flaws are much harder to change.

TOXICITY IS A PATTERN.

11. The Zahir

Paulo Coelho, Pg 207

"In order for the true energy of love to penetrate your soul, your soul must be as if you had just been born."

Love thrives in a heart that is open and unencumbered by previous experiences. Holding onto past disappointments can obstruct future happiness. Embracing change is essential for moving forward.

When we allow love to blossom, it flourishes in a heart free from the burdens of past hurts and failures. Clinging to old emotional baggage, such as heartbreak, regret, or unresolved issues, can create barriers that block new opportunities. Genuine love, in all its forms, demands the bravery to release the past, heal, and fully engage with the present without the shadows of previous experiences looming over us.

Similarly, our journey to success is often stifled not by outside factors but by our reluctance to let go of past mistakes. The anxiety of repeating errors can trap us in cycles of doubt and hesitation. Yet, actual growth stems from our ability to reinvent ourselves—learning from experiences, adapting, and redefining our paths. Each setback offers valuable lessons, and every closed door paves the way for new opportunities. Progress isn't about dodging failure but transforming it into a foundation for something even better.

LOVE AND GROWTH HAPPEN WHEN WE RELEASE THE PAST.

12. The Liberation of Sita

Volga, Pg 13

Surpanakha to Sita (referring to Sudhira)

"I've realized that the meaning of success for a woman does not lie in her relationship with a man. Only after that realization, did I find this man's companionship."

Personal fulfilment should take precedence over the pursuit of companionship. Independence plays a crucial role. Individuals need to develop their identities before engaging in partnerships; they should achieve personal success before looking for a partner. A genuinely satisfying relationship arises from two complete individuals who are not looking for someone to fill a void but to enhance each other's lives. Independence is the foundation for a solid relationship—one must first nurture one's identity, goals, and sense of purpose before intertwining one's journey with someone else. When people succeed in various aspects of life—emotional, professional, or intellectual—they enter relationships as equals, contributing value instead of seeking approval. Only by standing firm in their own identity can individuals truly share their lives with another without losing themselves along the way.

Despite being academically equipped to move ahead professionally, I chose to get married at the age of 22. The years that followed subconsciously made me feel obligated because I was the dependent in the marriage, and in no time, I had lost my voice to object or refuse. It was only once I started working that I realized the difference. Self-care empowers you. Another lesson I want to share from my experience is that being independent helps you make decisions faster. In my case, I kept being in a relationship out of fear of the outside world. You can move out of a situation/ relationship if you can support yourself.

FULFILMENT COMES FROM SELF-SUFFICIENCY.

13. Living Spirituality

Meetu Bisht, Pg 73

"And till we have fully learnt the lesson that is trying to be imparted, certain patterns in our life keep repeating themselves."

Life's recurring challenges aren't meant to be punishments; they serve as valuable lessons. We keep encountering the same hurdles until we truly understand them. I've seen that these challenges persist until we learn to adapt. The true measure of our growth lies in our ability to evolve.

I was in a bad marriage, but why was I there – for the love of status, financial and social. I wanted a comfortable life but sans hard work. When I reflected on why I kept attracting a particular set of people in the past I realized that at the bottom of it was my love for status, popularity, and materialistic pleasures. There is no harm in having such desires. The problem is when you do not want to work for it and want them for free. They say, "There are no free meals in this world." Sometimes losing your voice, your respect is the price you land up paying. I learnt my lesson. And that changed my script.

GROWTH IS MEASURED BY HOW WELL WE EVOLVE, NOT HOW OFTEN WE AVOID.

PARENTING AND FAMILY

14. Conscious Parenting

Lee Lozowick, Pg 229

"The first things to keep in mind when talking to children is to consider them, at every age, to be fully cognizant, and deserving of the kind of respect that we would to get as adults, and that we would advance towards other adults whom we respect."

Showing respect to children strengthens our connections with them.

Many adults often overlook the intelligence and insight of children, mistakenly believing they are too young to understand complex emotions or situations. Children are much more observant and intuitive than we typically acknowledge. Effective parenting involves being mindful and patient and recognizing that our words and actions influence our perspective on the world.

By treating them as capable individuals—listening to their thoughts, acknowledging their feelings, and encouraging their self-expression—we help build their confidence, emotional intelligence, and future relationship skills. Respecting children doesn't mean giving up authority; instead, it's about guiding them with empathy, understanding, and the conviction that they deserve to be heard and appreciated.

It happened so many years ago when my son was in junior school; I received a call from the school saying, "He was found cheating." I was asked to meet the Headmistress the next day. When he returned from school, I waited for him to change and finish his lunch, and then we sat down to talk about the incident. I simply asked him, "Did you cheat or not?" His answer was, "Mamma, I was carrying a page with difficult spellings to revise before the examination, but when I took out my writing board and pencil box from the school bag, that page too got pulled out as it was kept on top of all the books in the bag. It fell on the floor, and the boy behind me complained to the teacher."

Me: Did you cheat?

Him: No

That was it. The next day, I met the Headmistress, narrated the incident, and told her I trusted my son. She called for his answer script and said, "His answer script will be checked because I trust your trust."

I am sure he did not cheat, but that made him realize the value of trust.

RESPECT NURTURES TRUST.

15. Unposted Letter

The Voice of Ra, Pg 13

"For our children, we are the only Koran they
will read in their lifetime;
the only Vedas they will see;
the only Bible they will experience;
the only Dharma they will follow.

Your life and my life will either serve
as a Warning or as an Example."

Kids absorb lessons more from what they see than from what they hear. In my experiences with mentoring teams and parenting, I've understood that demonstrating the right behaviour is far more impactful than simply giving advice.

Whether it's about brushing their teeth at night, sticking to a bedtime, avoiding sugary drinks, or enjoying a book before sleep, I didn't explicitly teach them these habits—they learned by watching me.

ACTIONS SHAPE LESSONS THAT WORDS CANNOT.

16. The Conscious Parent

Shefali Tsabary, Pg 226

"Everything can't be a rule. A house with too many rules will simply fall apart one day. Children who are brought up with an undue amount of rules, with insufficient free space to explore and experiment, are likely to swing to the wild side, unable to metabolize their parents' rigidity any longer."

Children require direction, yet they also benefit from the freedom to discover. Excessive rules can hinder their creativity and sense of independence. I've observed that too much structure can restrict imaginative thinking. Providing a supportive framework is important while granting them the liberty to create and explore.

In grade 11, my son decided to opt for Arts, and I did not interfere with the choice, but asked for a plan - what he intends to do with the subjects and what he plans to do after grade 12. I gave him 6 months to come back with the answers. Coming from a middle-class family, it was important for us to have a plan to take the necessary guidance and action. He was as confused as he was 6 months earlier, so based on his interests, I suggested Law. He agreed and started preparing for the entrance exam while in school. I did the research and shortlisted colleges for applications. He cracked the entrance at IIM Rohtak right after grade 12 and is now pursuing a BBA LLB from the only IIM in India that offers a law program. Giving him the freedom to choose a subject and to plan the journey ahead was something that he appreciated, and following my guidance is what I appreciate about him. Together, we achieved what we aimed for.

BALANCE BETWEEN RULES- GUIDANCE AND FREEDOM IS THE KEY TO UNLOCKING POTENTIAL.

17. Family Reflections and Memories

Jane P. Resnick

"Nonetheless, I admire parents who insist upon responsible behaviour from their children and then follow through by letting the kids suffer the consequences of their irresponsibility. A friend of mine, without exception, insists that if her children oversleep and miss the bus, they walk the three miles to school. If they forget the necessary clothing, they get wet in the rain, freeze in the snow, or bake in the sun."

Instilling responsibility through consequences rather than overprotection fosters independence and real-world readiness.

It isn't about micromanaging—it's about setting expectations and letting children own their successes and failures.

From losing a debate to winning the school election to getting into IIM, I have only been a supporter, cheerleader, and critic, but I do not take credit or blame myself. My son learnt to own his wins and losses early on.

RESPONSIBILITY COMES FROM OWNERSHIP OF VICTORIES AND SETBACKS.

18. Parenting Teens in Modern Times

Anju Musafir-Chazot Pg 126

"Helping teenagers structure their personal time with hobbies, reading or even constructive self-reflection will help them use their 'alone' time better."

Adolescence is a critical period for identity formation and emotional regulation. Engaging in hobbies or reading can enhance cognitive development and emotional intelligence, while self-reflection can promote self-awareness.

Structured personal time encourages lifelong learning, critical thinking, and creativity, helping teenagers develop skills that aid academic and personal success.

Parents might view this as a way to keep their children engaged in meaningful activities, reducing excessive screen time or negative influences.

Some teens may resist structured time, valuing their freedom. However, if they find hobbies or books that truly interest them, they might see this structure as a way to explore passions and independence.

Introducing Badminton, Skating, Basketball, Football, Swimming, Painting, and Reading not only made them sensitive and emotionally and physically stronger but on days when we did not step out of the house, did not go out on vacations, I never heard them saying – "Mamma, we are getting bored."

STRUCTURED HOBBIES FOSTER GROWTH.

19. The Algebra of Happiness

Scott Galloway

"Raising kids with someone who is kind and competent and who you enjoy being with is a series of joyous moments smothered in comfort and reward. Raising kids with someone you don't like, or who isn't competent, is moments of joy smothered in anxiety and disappointment."

This quote serves as a powerful reminder that the individuals you choose to share your life with significantly influence the emotional landscape of your existence. Relationships, particularly with a partner, can provide a haven or create ongoing turmoil. A supportive partnership enhances joy and brings comfort to daily life. At the same time, a detrimental one can sap your energy and turn moments of happiness into brief respites from stress and dissatisfaction. Ultimately, the most crucial decision in life revolves not just around who you are with but how that person impacts your feelings daily.

This idea resonates with me beyond romantic connections and applies to professional and personal relationships, friendships, and collaborations. Whether collaborating with mentors who inspire and guide you or being part of teams that appreciate and enhance each other's strengths, the outcome remains the same: comfort, joy, and personal growth. I've noticed that you flourish when surrounded by kind, capable, and genuinely invested individuals. Conversely, even achievements can feel burdensome when instability or negativity is part of the mix. This reminds me to make thoughtful choices—people are not merely companions; they significantly influence the quality of your everyday life.

A partner continuously reminding you of your incapability and trying to find flaws with how you dress or speak would eventually make you believe you are not good enough. And have you ever seen unhappy parents raise happy children?

THE PEOPLE WE CHOOSE SHAPE OUR EMOTIONAL WORLD.

MONEY AND CAREER

20. Rich Dad Poor Dad

Robert T. Kiyosaki, Pg 217

"LESSON 6: WORK TO LEARN – DON'T WORK FOR MONEY

Job security meant everything to my educated dad
Learning meant everything to my rich dad."

Skills and knowledge hold greater value than money.

I've gained valuable lessons throughout my career, whether in hospitality or academia. In the long term, the ability to learn and adapt has proven to be far more important than a paycheck. Over the years, I have spent much time perfecting the art of storytelling. Be it short courses, reading, or following the leaders in the workspace, I have never shirked from learning at work. It has not only strengthened my resume but also kept me productively occupied.

INVESTING IN LEARNING PAYS THE HIGHEST DIVIDENDS.

21. Die With Zero

Bell Perkins, Pg 121

"Nothing has a greater effect on your ability to enjoy experiences – at any age – than your health. In fact, health is actually a lot more valuable than money, because no amount of money can ever make up for very poor health – whereas people in good health but with little money can still have many wonderful experiences."

Health plays a more crucial role in our quality of life than wealth ever can. I've observed many individuals pursuing their careers at the expense of their well-being. However, what is the value of success if you're too worn out to appreciate it?

Incorporating Yoga into my daily routine opened my eyes to the fact that I needed a healthy mind and body to truly excel and challenge myself. As the saying goes, there are many types of problems, but health issues all boil down to one significant concern.

ACHIEVEMENT BEGINS WITH A STRONG MIND AND BODY.

22. You Can Win

Shiv Khera, Pg 83

"Preparation is the necessary edge to succeed in any field.

Purpose + Principle + Planning + Practice + Perseverance + Patience + Pride = Preparation

Preparation leads to Confidence"

Success is not merely a matter of luck; it stems from thorough preparation. Although luck can sometimes influence outcomes, genuine and enduring success is rooted in hard work, determination, and strategic foresight. Each accomplishment arises from meticulous planning, wise choices, and the capacity to navigate obstacles. Individuals who invest time and effort in preparation are the ones who forge their paths, transforming hard work into outstanding results and dreams into tangible achievements.

I had no prior experience when I joined Marriott, and some might attribute it to good fortune. However, the subsequent achievements were not just a product of luck; they resulted from dedication and perseverance.

LUCK MIGHT OPEN A DOOR, BUT PREPARATION AND PERSISTENCE LEAD TO GUARANTEED SUCCESS.

23. Rules of the Game

Sumit D Chowdhury, Pg 70

1. *"Communication is about selling an idea and rallying people to execute.*
2. *Good communication is an acquired skill, so work on it.*
3. *What you speak and how you speak, changes the potential impact.*
4. *Listen first, analyze next and speak after – only if you have something to say."*

Effective communication is not something we are born with; it is a skill we develop over time. It involves intentional practice and a thorough understanding of how our words, tone, and context influence our interactions. Clarity is essential for ensuring our message is received as we intend, while empathy helps us connect with others by recognizing their feelings and viewpoints. Additionally, timing is vital—selecting the appropriate moment to express ourselves can influence whether our words bring healing, motivation, or discord. How we communicate is just as important as the content itself. A message shared with kindness and authenticity can foster trust, whereas the same message delivered thoughtlessly may lead to confusion. To truly master communication, we must pay attention to what we say and how we say it, aiming to create connections rather than divisions.

COMMUNICATION IS AN ART THAT CAN TURN WORDS INTO MEANINGFUL CONNECTIONS.

24. Negotiating Secrets

David Brown, Pg 48-49

"The power of silence. Never forget the power of a pause.

You've got two ears and one mouth. Use them in that proportion" German proverb."

Communication is more than just exchanging words; it's about truly understanding the person in front of you. It's not just about speaking clearly or articulating your thoughts—it's about creating a connection. Real communication happens when both parties feel heard, respected, and understood. That's where *active listening* comes in.

Active listening goes beyond nodding or waiting for your turn to speak. It means being fully present in the conversation, picking up on tone, body language, and the emotions behind the words. It's about asking thoughtful questions, reflecting on what you've heard, and showing empathy. When we genuinely listen, we build trust. We make people feel seen and valued. Being a good listener sets the foundation for deeper and more meaningful connections, whether in a professional setting, a personal relationship, or a casual chat. And here's the thing—people remember how you made them feel. They remember if you paid attention and made them feel heard.

In a world where everyone's eager to speak, the ones who *listen* stand out. Being a good listener is not just a nice-to-have—it's a superpower.

COMMUNICATION ALSO MEANS "MAKING PEOPLE FEEL HEARD".

25. You Can Negotiate

Herb Cohen, Pg 16

"Power is a mind-blowing entity. It's the capacity or ability to get things done...to exercise control over people, events, situations, and oneself. However, all power is based on perception. If you think you've got it, then you've got it. If you think you don't have it, even if you have it, then you don't have it."

Confidence is more than just a trait; it's a mindset that drives personal growth, resilience, and advancement. At its essence, confidence is influenced not by the extent of your knowledge but by the strength of your belief in your ability to learn, adapt, and overcome challenges. That inner voice reassuring you, "I might not have all the answers now, but I believe I can find them."

Genuine confidence isn't about being flawless or always correct. It arises from your readiness to show up, to try again after facing obstacles, and to persist even in uncertain times. It develops gradually through experiences, small victories, and even setbacks that reveal our potential to achieve more than we thought possible.

When you trust your skills, you pave the way for growth and unlock opportunities previously unnoticed. So don't wait until you feel completely prepared. Embrace the challenge. Have faith in your journey. Support yourself, and everything else will fall into place.

During one of the work assignments, I had to assist the Donor department (I am a Marketing and Communications professional). The first thing I did was an online course in fundraising from Berkeley Haas. I wanted to hit the ground running. And extra knowledge never hurts.

CONFIDENCE IS ABOUT YOUR ABILITY TO LEARN AND ADAPT.

26. Do Epic Shit

Ankur Warikoo, Pg 96

"Who you spend time with will define the stories you hear.
The stories you hear will define the stories in your head.
The stories in your head will define you.
Choose who you spend time, wisely!"

This quote expresses a simple yet profound truth: we are shaped by the voices we surround ourselves with. The narratives others share influence the stories we tell ourselves, forming our beliefs and impacting our decisions, confidence, and aspirations. By surrounding yourself with individuals who inspire, challenge, and uplift you, you enhance your life and transform your inner dialogue, ultimately determining the person you become. It's essential to make thoughtful choices about your circle, as your community plays a significant role in crafting your story.

I have intentionally distanced myself from negative individuals. This doesn't mean I'm unwilling to help; I recognize that maintaining a positive mindset with work and family responsibilities is crucial. Negative people often cling to their habits and can drain your energy, and I cannot afford to lose my spark. If someone perceives me as selfish for this choice, so be it.

I remember having a colleague who had a problem with everything at the workplace, and very soon, I started feeling the same. However, in my next role, I had many happy people who would share funny reels and not office/HR memes on Instagram with me, and I started looking forward to being at work even on days when I did not feel well.

CHOOSE VOICES THAT INSPIRE AND UPLIFT.

27. Atomic Habits

James Clear, Pg 123

"One of the most effective things you can do to build better habits is to join a culture where (1) your desired behavior is the normal behavior and (2) you already have something in common with the group."

Habits flourish in the company of others; they are influenced by the environments we choose to be part of. By surrounding yourself with individuals for whom your desired habits come naturally, adapting to those habits becomes easier and feels more instinctive. When you connect with that group, the transition feels less like a struggle and more like a sense of belonging. Culture is a powerful driver for change — by creating or joining the right one, you've already won half the battle.

This idea resonates strongly with my career path. I've naturally raised my expectations in environments where excellence, curiosity, and integrity are the standard. I've discovered that the right communities motivate you to develop habits and integrate them into your identity. Interacting with cultures that mirror your goals is not just a smart move — it's a form of self-care.

SURROUND YOURSELF WITH EXCELLENCE AND GROWTH BECOMES SECOND NATURE.

28. Whale Done!

Ken Blanchard, Pg 40

"The WHALE DONE Response

1. *Praise people immediately.*
2. *Be specific about what they did right or almost right.*
3. *Share your positive feelings about what they did.*
4. *Encourage them to keep up the good work."*

Positive reinforcement can be incredibly effective. People flourish when they receive recognition, not only for achieving perfection but also for making significant progress toward it. Offering immediate and specific praise fosters confidence, trust, and motivation. It's important to go beyond a simple "good job" and highlight precisely what someone did well and how it impacted you, so they understand what behaviours to continue.

In both my professional and personal life, I've witnessed the profound impact of encouragement, particularly when it's timely, clear, and sincere. While saying "well done" is nice, going the extra mile with enthusiastic praise—acknowledging specific actions, expressing how those actions made a difference, and encouraging them to keep pushing forward—creates a truly magical effect. I strive to implement this approach with my teams and colleagues, as it enhances performance and fosters trust and a sense of belonging.

During my first job, I encountered extremely encouraging bosses; receiving a lip colour for doing a creative (my job) or sending a message over the mail reading – You are a STAR… made me do my work enthusiastically.

RECOGNITION TURNS PROGRESS INTO LASTING MOTIVATION.

MINDFULNESS, POSITIVITY, HAPPINESS

29. Live Life in Crescendo

Stephen R. Covey and Cynthia Covey Haller, Pg 163

"1. *Understand the gravest problems are finite, and your choices are infinite*
2. *Leave the past behind – live in the moment*
3. *Choose optimism and a positive outlook*

"Gratitude makes optimism sustainable. And if you don't think you have anything to be grateful for, keep looking." – Michael J. Fox"

Gratitude serves as the cornerstone of optimism. The most effective marketing strategies and life decisions arise from a place of thankfulness, transforming our viewpoint from scarcity to abundance.

Thanks to my parents' support, my children could attend excellent schools, and I felt a strong desire to express my gratitude to the Universe in return. I always believed I would have found a way to support my children's education even without my parents' assistance. However, since they covered the tuition for one of my children, it was my duty to ensure another child's education outside my family. I did this not as an act of charity but as a gesture of gratitude.

ACKNOWLEDGE ABUNDANCE AND MORE GETS CREATED.

30. It Ends With Us

Colleen Hoover, Pg 367

"You can stop swimming now, Lily. We finally reached the shore."

Understanding when our challenges have ended is as important as finding the strength to overcome them. We often become so accustomed to pushing ahead that we forget to take a moment to pause, breathe, and recognize that the difficult times are behind us.

I've come to understand that resilience is not just about enduring tough times; it's also about celebrating our progress. It's about appreciating the stillness that follows the chaos and the peace that comes after the busyness.

Reflecting on how far we've travelled is not a sign of selfishness; it's essential. It helps us acknowledge our growth, recognize our healing, and cultivate gratitude.

I've realized it's perfectly fine to pause and say, "That was tough, but I got through it." Instead of rushing into the next objective, I'm learning to savour my achievements. I want to recognize the big and small victories and give them the recognition they deserve.

RESILIENCE ALSO MEANS

- RECOGNIZING THAT THE STORM HAS PASSED
- EMBRACING THE CALM

31. Zen and the Art of Happiness

Chris Prentiss, Pg 3

"There is only one way to achieve lasting happiness, that way is simply: Be happy."

Happiness is a decision, not merely a consequence of our circumstances. It doesn't hinge on landing the perfect job, finding the ideal partner, or having a specific amount in your bank account. It starts in our minds. Each day, we can choose our outlook — to view obstacles as hindrances or opportunities for growth.

Fostering a positive mindset is essential for enduring happiness. It's not about dismissing the tough times but rather about learning to handle them with poise. It involves training your mind to discover light even in the most challenging situations.

In marketing, we promote dreams — the ideal lifestyle, the ultimate solution, the sensation of having 'made it.' In research, we delve into understanding what motivates people, what influences behaviour, and what fosters connections.

Yet, in our lives, we often overlook these truths. We forget to pause between achievements, to appreciate progress rather than perfection, and to recognize the beauty in the present moment. We pursue our goals, and in doing so, we sometimes overlook the joy that comes from simply existing.

So today, choose to embrace happiness. Not because everything is flawless, but because you deserve to relish the journey, not just the end goal.

MAKE "I AM HAPPY" A DAILY CONSCIOUS CHOICE.

32. The Magic

Rhonda Byrne, Pg 124

"Gratitude is something you must have before you can receive it, not something that you simply do after something good has happened. Most people are grateful after they receive something good, but to make all your wishes come true and change your entire life by filling it with riches in every area, you must be grateful before and after."

Expressing gratitude in advance paves the way for abundance. It involves transforming our perspective from one of scarcity to one of fulfilment. By showing appreciation for what we currently possess and our future aspirations, we communicate a strong message—to ourselves and the Universe—that we are open to receiving.

In the realm of public relations and branding, I have witnessed the remarkable effects of this principle. When we sincerely value individuals, their narratives, and their contributions before seeking anything in return, we establish a foundation of trust. This trust is essential for building stronger, more genuine relationships.

The same concept holds in life. Whether in friendships, opportunities, or dreams, we create room for meaningful connections and delightful surprises when we express appreciation before having expectations. Gratitude is not a passive act but an active, magnetic force that transforms our intentions into reality.

So, let's embrace a mindset of thankfulness in our daily lives. The outcome? Deeper connections, richer experiences, and a sense of fulfilment—well before our goals are achieved.

GRATITUDE IS THE SHORTCUT TO MANIFESTING EVERYTHING THAT YOU SEEK IN LIFE.

33. The Power

Rhonda Byrne Pg 181

"The law of attraction is responding to your feelings. Whatever you give, you receive, and so if you stick a label on any person, circumstance, or event in life, you are sticking the label on you, and that's what you will receive."

Energy operates reciprocally. What you put out into the world is what you receive in return. When you concentrate on positivity, hope, and kindness, those qualities manifest more frequently in your life. Positivity has a magnetic effect; it elevates your spirit and attracts the right people and opportunities to you.

Conversely, negativity functions in a similar way. If you linger in doubt, criticism, or cynicism, those feelings will reflect on you.

Branding follows the same principle. It goes beyond just a logo or a catchy phrase; it's about how you are perceived. How you present yourself and what you consistently communicate shapes your brand, which draws in those who connect with it.

I've come to understand that this concept applies not only to businesses but to individuals as well.

We are all living brands, subtly conveying our identity through energy, actions, and presence. So, consider this: What message are you sending out? And what are you inviting into your life?

ENERGY IS A MIRROR, BE MINDFUL OF WHAT YOU RADIATE.

34. A Little Book of Happiness

Ruskin Bond

"Happiness does not arrive with fireworks. It settles in quietly, long before you recognize it. And sometimes it is gone before you do."

True happiness isn't dramatic; it's subtle and often unnoticed.

It's not always found in the loud celebrations or grand achievements.

It hides in the quiet satisfaction after a task well done, the warmth of a kind message, the stillness of early mornings, and the laughter between meetings.

In both work and life, we often chase the "big moment" — the promotion, the milestone, the applause.

But real joy often shows up in the mundane:

A good conversation, a shared coffee, an unexpected compliment, a peaceful evening.

The small moments matter.

They're the threads that weave a truly fulfilling life.

Pause. Notice. Appreciate.

Because happiness isn't always an event — sometimes, it's a whisper.

A co-worker leaving a candy packet every week on my desk, flowers in the lobby of the hotel where I worked, "You have a lovely smile" from a guest who was checking out, or a reply on my WhatsApp status from my contacts saying, "This made my day!", all of these qualify as my super happy moments in a day.

HAPPINESS IS NOT ALWAYS LOUD.

35. The Saint The Surfer And The CEO

Robin Sharma, Pg 189

"You will be happy in your life in direct proportion to the degree to which you will be helpful to the world."

True happiness isn't found in chasing personal milestones alone but in how much value we add to others' lives. The more we shift focus from 'What do I get?' to 'How can I help?' — the more fulfilled we become. Contribution multiplies joy. In being useful, we find purpose, and purpose anchors happiness.

The joy of connecting people to opportunities, creating something lasting, or simply solving someone's problem has always been my true currency of happiness. Giving isn't a detour from success; it's the core road to fulfilment.

How can sharing - where you bought that bag or dress from, what hobby classes your daughter attends, or which courses to take to learn about coding- ever hurt?

TRUE JOY COMES FROM GENEROSITY.

36. Know Yourself Help Yourself

Practical Ways to a Powerful Personality

George Weinberg, Pg 31

"First, never belittle other people for their emotional reactions, no matter what they are; and if they talk about being angry or annoyed with someone, don't make the mistake of concluding that they necessarily dislike the person.

The second is, hold yourself accountable for all your decisions. ..."

We often impose an unspoken expectation of emotional perfection on ourselves, believing we should only experience feelings deemed "appropriate" or "positive." However, emotions do not adhere to set rules; they simply exist. Many of us criticize our feelings—frustration, jealousy, sadness, or even joy. We tell ourselves that we shouldn't experience these emotions, creating a gap between our true selves and the ideal version we should embody.

Yet, personal growth starts with embracing reality, not denying it.

Recognizing your emotions without attaching guilt or self-criticism is the foundation of genuine self-awareness. It's not about giving in to every feeling or allowing them to control your actions; it's about acknowledging them, identifying them, and granting yourself the freedom to experience them. Emotions are not weaknesses; they are valuable information and messengers. By paying attention to them, we gain insights.

What truly matters is not whether we feel emotions, but how we respond to them. Taking responsibility means owning our actions rather than blaming ourselves for our natural reactions. It's both possible and empowering to acknowledge. "Yes, I felt that. Here's how I chose to respond, regardless of those feelings."

However, the more I permitted myself to feel without judgment, the easier it became to distinguish my emotions from my choices.

EMOTIONS ARE INSIGHTS. EMBRACE THEM WITHOUT GUILT OR DENIAL.

37. When Bad Things Happen to Good People

Harold S. Kushner, Pg xiv

"...we cannot choose. We can only try to cope. That is what one does with sorrow, with tragedy, with any misfortune. We do not try to explain it. We do not justify it by telling ourselves that we somehow deserve it. We do not even accept it. We survive it. We recognize its unfairness and defiantly choose to go on living."

Some things in life will never make sense — no logic, reason, or fairness. However, the most potent response is not to justify or accept these moments but to survive them. Survival, in this case, is an act of defiance. It's saying, "I may not have chosen this, but I choose to keep going." That resilience is where strength quietly lives.

This resonates so deeply. Whether it's life throwing curveballs personally or professionally, I've realized — not everything demands understanding or acceptance. Some losses, failures, or unfair moments are just that: unfair. But what I *can* choose every single time is to move forward with grace. Survival and resilience aren't passive responses; they're bold decisions we repeatedly make when the world is loud, and we need to be louder in our quiet strength.

I am far from being a company's CMO, but creating an identity for myself as a marketing professional in the last 7 years is my story of survival, and I am proud of it.

CHOOSING TO FIGHT FOR SURVIVAL IS A SUCCESS STORY IN MAKING.

SPIRITUALITY, PERSPECTIVE, PURPOSE

38. It's Your Life

Vinita Dawra Nangia, Pg 92

"Must you understand everything?

Life would be much simpler and happier if we stopped trying to understand everything and just moved on, focused on understanding ourselves instead!"

Not everything requires a solution—what truly matters is self-awareness. It's easy to become engrossed in finding answers, attempting to decode every enigma or make sense of every circumstance. However, I've come to understand that true strength lies not in possessing all the answers but in knowing myself—acknowledging my values, emotions, and instincts. When we root ourselves in self-awareness, we can face life's uncertainties with clarity, even when the way ahead is unclear.

I yearn for understanding, yet I've also realized that sometimes, releasing the need to know 'why' can bring tranquility. The desire to comprehend everything can lead to anxiety. We find ourselves questioning intentions, seeking explanations, and straining to connect the dots. But I've learned that the peace I seek often arises not from having an answer but simply letting go of the need for one. There is solace in recognizing that not all questions have quick answers and that some experiences are meant to be lived rather than understood. By relinquishing the 'why,' we open space for peace, trust, and the freedom to simply exist.

IT IS LIBERATING TO LEARN THAT NOT EVERYTHING NEEDS TO BE UNDERSTOOD.

39. Don't Worry

Shunmyo Masuno, Pg 95

"No matter how capable you might think you are, there is a natural limit to what you can accomplish on your own."

"Learn to be grateful that whatever work you do is supported by others."

Our lives are shaped by the countless generations preceding us, whose choices, sacrifices, and actions have moulded our world today. It's easy to overlook that we benefit from the groundwork laid by those who came before us. However, taking a moment to appreciate their contributions can enhance our gratitude and broaden our perspective. Every achievement we celebrate—whether in our personal endeavours or professional paths—rests on the foundation established by others, including our families, mentors, colleagues, and society. Recognizing this interconnectedness highlights the importance of collaboration and shared experiences and keeps us grounded, humble, and aware of the larger context. Our journey is never solely our own; it is a collective endeavour that merits acknowledgement.

This reminds me of Smriti, who helped me during Geography practicals in college; Shiuli, who taught me Python; Raman, who would format my presentations; Shelly, who would soak flax seeds for me just because I mentioned, back home, I would have them early in the morning...

ACKNOWLEDGE AND REMEMBER WHO SUPPORTED YOU IN YOUR JOURNEY.

40. When Things Fall Apart

Pema Chodron, Pg 103

Widening the circle of compassion - Chapter 13

"Only in an open, nonjudgemental space can we acknowledge what we are feeling. Only in an open space where we're not all caught up in our own version of reality can we see and hear and feel who others really are, which allows us to be with them and communicate with them properly."

Genuine understanding stems from approaching situations with an open mind and a non-judgmental perspective. Listening without preconceived ideas or biases paves the way for deeper connections and more significant insights. In our personal and professional lives, it's important to acknowledge that everyone brings their unique experiences, viewpoints, and feelings to the conversation. By welcoming this diversity and avoiding hasty judgments, we foster a richer and more authentic comprehension of others.

In any relationship—professional or personal—the key to success lies in empathy and open communication. Empathy enables us to genuinely understand another person's feelings, promoting compassion and mutual respect. Meanwhile, open communication ensures that discussions are clear and fluid, allowing both sides to feel acknowledged and appreciated. Together, these traits cultivate trust and collaboration, where teamwork flourishes, and conflicts are handled with respect and understanding.

By maintaining an open and non-judgmental stance, we enhance our relationships and help create an environment where growth, creativity, and understanding thrive. Through this openness, we unlock the potential for stronger, more resilient connections across all aspects of life.

GIVE EVERYONE A CHANCE BEFORE YOU FORM AN OPINION BASED ON OTHERS OR 'ONE' INCIDENT.

41. A Bowl of Chicken Soup for the Soul

Jack Canfield, Mark Victor Hansen

"I learned, facing backwards, that life meant more than just survival.

My success was in my journey, not in my arrival."

Success is not merely a destination; it's a journey influenced by the experiences and personal development we undergo. In every area of our lives—whether in our careers, studies, or personal projects—the journey of striving, learning, and growing holds far greater significance than the result. While achievements are valuable, they are overshadowed by the personal growth we gain while pursuing them. We truly understand what success means through facing challenges, overcoming obstacles, and learning from our experiences. Each small step forward is a triumph in its own right. In the end, it is our growth, resilience, and the insights we acquire that truly define success, not just our final destination but the individuals we become throughout the journey.

EVERY STEP FORWARD IS ALSO SUCCESS.

42. Messages From The Masters

Dr. Brian Weiss, Pg 108-109

"It is extremely important to pay serious attention to the coincidences, the synchronicities, and the déjà vu experiences in our lives because they often represent the convergence of our spiritual plan and the actual path we are travelling during our lifetime."

Life is brimming with signs, just waiting for us to notice them, provided we keep our minds open. Each experience, interaction, and what may seem like a random occurrence carries a deeper significance. By being attentive, these instances can illuminate our path, guiding us toward our true purpose.

Reflecting on my journey, I've learned that unexpected opportunities often steer our lives in ways we never anticipated. These moments are when life gently pushes us, presenting new directions or uncovering hidden paths that foster growth, learning, and a richer understanding of who we are.

Frequently, what we label as a "coincidence" is merely life communicating with us, sending a message, inviting us to take a risk, or reminding us that we are precisely where we need to be, even if it doesn't seem that way. If we listen and trust these signs, we can unlock the potential to lead a life filled with purpose, significance, and connection. It's all there in the subtle nudges and whispers—if we are prepared to acknowledge them.

COINCIDENCES ARE SIGNS. PAY ATTENTION TO THEM.

43. Living a Life That Matters

Harold Kushner, Pg 166

"We matter, not because of our achievements but because we are loved by God and loved by the people around us. That love may not shield us from pain, death and loss, but it will make them more bearable, and that will be enough."

Success isn't just about the awards we receive, the projects we complete, or the recognition we gain. Real success is found in the relationships we cultivate, the trust we establish, and the love we share throughout our journey. While titles and accolades may be temporary and eventually fade, the deep and lasting influence we have on the lives of others is what truly matters. In branding, the connections we create with customers give a brand its enduring strength, going beyond mere first impressions. Likewise, in our personal lives, the relationships we nurture, the kindness we extend, and the love we express build our legacy. Ultimately, these connections define how we are remembered and the impact we make in the world. At its core, success is about the love we impart and the positive change we inspire in others.

ACHIEVEMENTS = LOVE THAT WE RECEIVE, KINDNESS WE EXHIBIT AND PEOPLE WHOSE LIVES WE TOUCHED

44. Nine Essential Things I've Learned about Life

Harold S. Kushner, Pg 101

"...the ability to know the difference between good and bad, between things that should be done and things that should not be done, the freedom no other creature has to use willpower to override temptation."

Life presents us with opportunities for fresh starts, and having faith—whether in a greater force or ourselves—can empower us to bounce back from setbacks. I've experienced changes in my career, faced obstacles, and embarked on new beginnings, yet each time, I've discovered my inner strength. It's not our mistakes that shape us, but rather the lessons we take from them.

Dealing with work demands and dynamics while being a single parent to two very young kids was no small achievement; despite my struggles, my professional path began in a way that few would expect, and I had no grounds for complaint. Today, I am respected by the people who know me not because of what I have, but who I am. My willpower and faith have helped me create a life that is fulfilling in every way. A proud mother, a fairly successful professional, and most importantly, a very strong, undeterred woman. From seeking help from my doctor for depression and thriving on antidepressants due to a failing marriage to helping women going through struggles in marriage and giving professional guidance, I have come a long way. There was always a temptation- not to act, to do nothing about the situation.

Whether you believe in "God" or not, the lesson remains: USE WILLPOWER, GIVE YOURSELF A SECOND CHANCE.

45. Bhagvad-Gita As It Is

His Divine Grace – AC Bhaktivedanta Swami Prabhupada, Pg 105

"A man must elevate himself by his own mind, not degrade himself. The mind is the friend of the conditioned soul, and his enemy as well.

For he who has conquered his mind, it is the best of friends; but for one who has failed to do so, his very mind will be the greatest enemy."

Teaching self-discipline is essential. A strong mindset can be your greatest ally, while a weak one may lead to self-sabotage.

The way we think can determine our success or failure. Achieving success involves training your mind to concentrate on long-term objectives rather than bogged down by short-term challenges.

Instilling self-discipline is one of the most important life lessons, as it builds character, resilience, and the capacity to face difficulties with determination. A strong, disciplined mind offers clarity, focus, and perseverance to tackle adversity. Conversely, a weak or undisciplined mind can become a significant obstacle, fostering self-doubt, procrastination, and hasty decisions that impede progress.

Mindset is the key element that can either elevate or hinder an individual. Genuine success stems not from luck or talent but from consistent effort, mental fortitude, and the ability to prioritize long-term aspirations over fleeting setbacks. Those who learn to manage their thoughts, emotions, and actions can navigate challenges gracefully, transforming failures into valuable lessons and obstacles into opportunities. Cultivating a disciplined mind is not about imposing restrictions but embracing the freedom to intentionally shape one's future.

SELF-DISCIPLINE IS THE MANTRA TO TACKLE CHALLENGES, HARDSHIPS AND DIFFICULTIES.

SELF-DISCIPLINE > STRONG MIND > FOCUS > SOLUTION

Acknowledgment

To Reema, my first friend, who taught me the true meaning of friendship before I even knew how to spell the word.

We met when we were just eight, when friendship wasn't about saying the right things but about simply being there—through every cutti-appa, every argument over candy wrappers, and every moment of unfiltered honesty. You were my friend when I refused to let you copy my geography notes in fourth grade, and you were still my friend when I relied on yours in fifth. You stood by me when I unfairly objected to you having other friends, and you fought for me when someone wronged me. You found ways to keep our friendship alive—suggesting we time our calls with Doordarshan news so I wouldn't get scolded, never minding when my Dadi disapproved of your endless energy. You were never deterred, never offended, always loving—always Reema.

You were the first to place an order when my first book was published. Your name wasn't in the acknowledgements, but you never mentioned it. That's who you are—whether I name you or not, you remain steadfastly there. But this book, "Borrowed Wisdom That Made Me Wise", is about learning, and the first lesson I ever learned—before books, before formal education—was through you. You taught me what friendship truly is.

So how could I not acknowledge you in a book about wisdom when you were my first teacher?

Thank you, Reema, for choosing me as your friend. My Gen Z daughter calls me a "snitch" and wonders how you're still my friend after all these stories. She doesn't know the how or the why—but I do. And I always will.

Special Acknowledgment

A heartfelt thank you to the brilliant authors whose works have been included in this compilation. Your words have inspired me and provided invaluable insights that have helped me navigate real-life situations with greater wisdom and clarity. Each book has been a guiding light, offering perspectives that challenge, uplift, and transform.

I highly recommend these books to everyone—whether for personal growth, professional development, or the joy of discovering new ideas. Your contributions to literature and thought are deeply appreciated!

About the Author

Vartika Dikshit is a seasoned marketing and communications professional with over seven years of experience in corporate communication, marketing, and operations. She has worked with renowned brands such as JW Marriott, Hyatt Hotels Corporation, ITC Hotels, Unison Education Foundation, Graphic Era University, and Taj Hotels. Her expertise spans hospitality, education, and wellness, where she has successfully led brand campaigns, media relations, and digital marketing strategies.

Vartika holds an MBA in Marketing and Human Resources, a gold medal in MA History, and a PhD in History, focusing on Tibetan Buddhism's influence in Dehradun.

She is the author of *Messfully Yours*, a book that blends humour and real-life chaos into an engaging narrative.

Known for her witty and compelling storytelling, Vartika enjoys crafting impactful brand narratives and developing innovative marketing strategies.

References

Backman, F. (2016). Britt-Marie Was Here. Sceptre.

Bharucha, R. N. (2010). The Fakir. Full Circle Books.

Bisht, M. (2021). Living Spirituality. Hay House Publishers India.

Blanchard, K. (2002). Whale Done! Free Pr.

Bond, R. (2016). A Little Book of Happiness. Speaking Tiger.

Brown, D. (2010). Negotiating Secrets. Collins.

Byrne, R. (2012). The Magic. Simon & Schuster.

Byrne, R. (2012). The Power. Simon & Schuster.

Canfield, J., & Hansen, M. V. (2012). A Bowl of Chicken Soup for the Soul. Blacklist LLC

Chodron, Pema. (2017). When Things Fall Apart. Harper Thorsons.

Clear, J. (2019). Atomic Habits. Yankeess.

Coelho, P. (2005). The Zahir. Harper.

Cohen, H. (2025). You Can Negotiate Anything. Jaico Publishing House.

Covey, S. R., & Haller, C. C. (2022). Live Life in Crescendo. Simon & Schuster.

De, S. (2012). Spouse. Penguin India.

Duckworth, A. (2017). Grit. Vermilion.

Galloway, S. (2019). The Algebra of Happiness. Random House.

Grover, D. (2024). Time to Come Home. Hay House Publishers India

Hoover, C. (2025). It Ends with Us. MikeyD

Khera, S. (2014). You Can Win. Bloomsbury

Kiyosaki, R. T. (2022). Rich Dad Poor Dad. Plata Publishing.

Kushner, H. S. (2011). Living a Life that Matters. Bluebird.

Kushner, H. S. (2016). Nine Essential Things I've Learned About Life. Anchor.

Kushner, H. S. (2004). When Bad Things Happen to Good People. Rhus.

Lozowick, L. (1996). Conscious Parenting. Hohm Press.

Mackesy, C. (2019). The Boy, The Mole, The Fox and The Horse. Ebury Press.

Masuno, S. (2022). Don't Worry. Michael Joseph.

Musafir-Chazot, A. (2013). Parenting Teens in Modern Times. Westland.

Nangia- Dawra, V. (2012). It's Your Life. Times Group.

Perkins, B. (2023). Die with Zero. Mariner Books.

Prabhupada, A. C. B. S. (2019). Bhagavad-Gita As It Is. The Bhaktivedanta Book Trust.

Prentiss, C. (2018). Zen and the Art of Happiness. Manjul Publishing House.

Ra, M. (2011). Unposted Letter. Manjul Publishing House.

Resnick, J. P. (1995). Family Reflections and Memories. Smithmark Pub.

Schuller, R. H. (2006). Believe in the God who Believes in You. Orient Paperbacks

Sharma, R. (2007). The Saint, the Surfer, and the CEO. Hay House.

Sharma, R. (2006). Who will cry when you die? Jaico Publishing House.

Soul, A. (2015). Reflections of a Man. Black Castle Media Group.

Sumit, D. C. (2014). Rules of the Game. Bloomsbury India P Ltd.

Tsabary, S. (2010). The Conscious Parent. Perseus Books Group.

Volga. (2018). The Liberation of Sita. Harper Perennial.

Warikoo, A. (2021). Do Epic Shit. Juggernaut Books.

Weinberg, G. (1975). Know Yourself Help Yourself. Sheldon Press.

Weiss, B. L. (1994). Many Lives, Many Masters. Piatkus.

Weiss, B. L. (2000). Messages from the Masters. Piatkus.

DISCLAIMER